Steve Parish

CELEBRATING AUSTRALIA

NATIONAL PARKS

Steve Parish

PUBLISHING

Preceding pages: Nandroya Falls, Wooroonooran National Park, Q; The Pinnacles, Nambung National Park, WA.

Above: Rainforest, Mt Warning National Park, NSW.

Introduction

Australia has been separated from all other continents for a very long time, and has been weathered into its own distinctive landscapes. It contains a wealth of habitats, from the arid deserts of the centre and north-west to the perpetually humid rainforests of the eastern coasts, and these habitats harbour many unique plants and animals.

The deserts of this driest of all the continents seem almost lifeless to those who fail to look at them closely, but at night they are full of life, and after rain they blossom with vivid wildflowers. In these deserts stand some of Australia's most remarkable landscape formations, such as Uluṟu and Kata Tjuṯa. In enormous contrast to the aridlands are the cool temperate and tropical rainforests, with their waterfalls, towering trees, ferns and palms. In between deserts and rainforests are eucalypt forests, plains, heathlands, mountain ranges and wetlands from rivers to billabongs. The Australian coastline, 36 000 kilometres in length, is an immensely varied collage of seascapes and shorescapes, offering such marvels as the Great Barrier Reef, the Whitsundays, the haunting limestone stacks of Port Campbell National Park and the wonderful beaches and headlands of southern Tasmania and Western Australia. Each of these environments has its own set of niches in which its particular plants and animals can flourish, and the most striking and best-loved of Australia's landscapes are protected in national parks.

When I travel the continent, I set a course from one national park to the next, anticipating the delights to come, realising that, like all other visitors, I must do my share to look after these fascinating reserves and ensure that they are there to be seen by generations to come.

This book celebrates some of Australia's most magnificent places.

Steve Parish

AUSTRALIA'S ARIDLANDS

Above: These sand dunes in the Simpson Desert appear void of life.

Opposite: After rain falls, the desert blossoms.

Australia's vast inland has been growing drier for millions of years. Once, dinosaurs roamed its swamps and plesiosaurs swam in its seas: today, the seas are sand and the lush vegetation has given way to drought-resistant eucalypts and acacias. The animals of the aridlands have also adapted to existing on very little water for considerable periods.

However, when rains come the desert blossoms. Dry bushes burst into leaf and flowers cover the red sands. Birds and other creatures produce young ones and plants set seed which will endure another dry spell, to bring forth new life after the next rains fall, perhaps years in the future.

Opposite: Wildflowers hint of life in the desert.   *Above:* Spinifex, the great aridland survivor.

Simpson Desert

The Birdsville Track stretches for 481 kilometres from the tiny town of Birdsville in Queensland to Marree in South Australia. On the way, it passes the eastern side of the Simpson Desert National Park, Queensland's largest at over 5000 square kilometres. Spinifex, native grasses and desert shrubs grow between long, high sand dunes, and summer temperatures are extreme. However, there is life in the desert, even in the dunes, and an early morning search will reveal countless tracks where small creatures have left their hiding places and searched for food in the cool of the night.

Rainbow Valley

Opposite: Cliff formations reflect the sunlight, dwarfing the surrounding landscape.

Above: Rainbow Valley after a dramatic thunderstorm.

Rainbow Valley, 101 kilometres south of Alice Springs in the Northern Territory, is best visited late in the afternoon. At this time, the brilliant rays of the setting sun shine onto the rugged cliffs of the James Range, the warm-hued sandstone glowing in rich tones of red and gold.

This small but magnificent conservation reserve is a well kept secret, perhaps because it is 22 kilometres off the Sturt Highway along a rough track. It is worth the effort of getting there, and camping overnight to watch sunset bring the valley walls to vibrant life, then to see the moon rise over the rugged range.

Uluṟu–Kata Tjuṯa

Above: The domes of Kata Tjuṯa rise in splendour from the plain.

Opposite: Uluṟu at dusk is a place of magic and mystery.

Two of the world's great natural wonders stand in Central Australia's Uluṟu–Kata Tjuṯa National Park, just under 500 kilometres south-west of Alice Springs. The great rock Uluṟu, 3.6 kilometres long, stands 348 metres above the plain. Kata Tjuṯa, a group of massive red domes 32 kilometres to the west, rises to 546 metres. The wild glory of these enormous landmarks fascinates all who witness their enormous size and watch their bewildering changes of colour at dusk and dawn.

Both formations are of great significance to the Aboriginal people, who lease the park to the Australian Nature Conservation Agency and take part in its administration.

Above: West MacDonnell National Park.

Opposite: Ormiston Gorge and Pound.

West MacDonnell

The rugged MacDonnell Ranges run for 400 kilometres west and east across Central Australia. Around 650 million years ago, they stood more than 3000 metres above sea level. Today, though weathered to much less than their former grandeur, they are still magnificent. Rivers have cut sheer-walled gorges in their multicoloured sandstone: in the shade of sheer cliffs lie pools of cool water, where wild creatures come to drink. The West MacDonnell Ranges stretch from Alice Springs westwards to Haasts Bluff, including unforgettable places such as Simpsons Gap, Standley Chasm, Glen Helen Gorge, Ormiston Gorge and Redbank Gorge.

The energetic can walk the backbone of the West MacDonnells along the Larapinta Trail, which stretches from Alice Springs to Mt Razorback, beyond Glen Helen. For others, there is excellent road access to the major beauty spots of these spectacular ranges.

Flinders Ranges

Above: Made blue by distance, the Flinders Ranges rise from undulating foothills.   *Opposite:* The Flinders Ranges framed by River Red Gums.

South Australia's Flinders Ranges begin some 250 kilometres north of Adelaide, then stretch for another 800 kilometres into the arid outback. They are Australia's most impressive range after the Great Divide, and offer limitless opportunities for nature lovers, bushwalkers and adventurers. Much of this wild and rugged area is reserved in Flinders Ranges National Park. It is especially popular with artists and photographers because of the kaleidoscopic range of colours which appear on slopes and cliffs as the sun crosses the sky. The Flinders Ranges are best seen in winter, when the weather is cooler, but the most rewarding landscapes occur in springtime, when wildflowers cover stark contours in brilliant colour.

Mungo

The "Walls of China" stretch for 30 kilometres in Mungo National Park, in the south-west corner of New South Wales.

Mungo National Park, within the Willandra Lakes World Heritage Region, is a 110 kilometre drive from Mildura, north-east into the desert. Around 40 000 years ago the Lachlan River flowed into Lake Mungo, and for 25 000 years the lake was a rich food source for Aboriginal people, who continue to live in the area. The lake has been dry for 15 000 years, its dry bed wind-shifted into crescent-shaped dunes or lunettes, known as the "Walls of China".

Wyperfeld

Long ago, Aboriginal people cut bark from this eucalypt.

The far north-western corner of Victoria is known as the Mallee, after the drought-resistant, tough-rooted eucalypt typical of the area. Wyperfeld National Park covers more than 356 000 hectares of mallee scrub and heathland south-west of Ouyen. This arid country nurtures more than 450 species of native plants and is rich in wildlife, with in excess of 200 bird species, including the Malleefowl, a rare mound-building bird.

Mt Augustus and Kennedy Range

Above: The Kennedy Range is a plateau dissected by wind and water into "jump-ups" which stretch for 200 kilometres.   *Opposite:* Mt Augustus.

Two of Western Australia's greatest aridland scenic attractions are the spectacular eroded plateau which forms the Kennedy Range, and the magnificent rock of Mt Augustus. Each of these features has its own national park boasting rugged beauty, abundant wildlife and interesting geology. Much of Kennedy Range National Park is still unexplored by Europeans and it is superb aridland wilderness. Mt Augustus is larger than Uluru, and is the world's greatest monolith, a huge mass which rises 1106 metres above sea level, its flanks clothed with mulga scrub.

Karijini

Above: Waterholes form focuses for wildlife in the Hamersley Range.

Opposite: The Pilbara landscape and the Hamersley Range.

It is nearly 300 kilometres from Port Hedland to Karijini National Park, which is centred on the breathtaking Hamersley Range in the Pilbara of Western Australia. Over countless ages, waterways have worn deep, steep-sided gorges into the iron-rich red rocks of the Hamersley Range: Dales Gorge, Weano Gorge, Red Gorge and Joffre Gorge are only four of many breathtakingly beautiful canyons in whose depths lie pools of cold, life-giving water. The spinifex-studded landscape of the surrounding plains blooms with wildflowers after rain.

THE TROPICAL NORTH

Australia's north is monsoon country, inundated by torrential rain each summer. During the wet season, the country becomes green and plants and animals reproduce before the bounty ceases and the dry season takes hold. The end of the Dry is marked by intense heat and a build-up of thunderstorms before the rainfalls of the Wet begin once more.

The north of Western Australia's Kimberley, the Northern Territory's Top End and Queensland's Gulf Country contain some of the world's remaining truly wild places. Luckily many of these are within the boundaries of national parks, protected for future generations to enjoy.

Fantastic rock formations in the proposed Limmen Gate National Park in the Northern Territory's Top End.

21

The Kimberley

Above: Bell Creek, in Bell Creek Reserve, tumbles into Bell Gorge.

Above: Geikie Gorge was formed by the Fitzroy River cutting into the limestone Geikie Range.

The western part of the Kimberley in Western Australia contains a number of well-known small national parks, such as Geikie and Windjana Gorges, and the incredible wilderness area of the Prince Regent Nature Reserve. In the central north is Drysdale River National Park, almost untouched by Europeans. Bell Creek, a tributary of the Isdell River, has its own reserve, around 230 kilometres from Derby.

Opposite: Windjana Gorge is a canyon 4 kilometres long cut by the Lennard River through a fossilised limestone reef.

Purnululu

Opposite: Rounded towers and domes, Purnululu National Park.

Above: The unusual rock formations of Purnululu National Park.

The awe-inspiring domes which are the major feature of Purnululu National Park, are tiger-striped in bands of orange, where the white sandstone has been stained with iron oxide, and grey-green shades of lichen. The park is in the north-west of the Kimberley in Western Australia, around five hours' travel by four-wheel-drive vehicle from Kununurra and four hours from Halls Creek. However, as the domes are fragile and the country difficult to traverse, the best way to see these remarkable formations is from a light aircraft. Known since Europeans first saw the area as the Bungle Bungles, Purnululu came to public notice only in 1983, and was proclaimed a national park in 1987.

Litchfield

Opposite: Florence Falls, Litchfield National Park.

Above: Magnetic Termite mounds are oriented north-south to remain cool in summer and warm in winter.

The 65 700-hectare Litchfield National Park is 100 kilometres from Darwin, capital of the Northern Territory, and encompasses part of the Tabletop Range. Impressive features include the magnificent waterfalls of Florence, Wangi, Tolmer and Tjaynera, the sandstone formations of the Lost City, and the tombstone-like Magnetic Termite mounds.

Kakadu

Above: The sandstone Arnhem Land Escarpment.   *Opposite*: Yellow Water, typical of Kakadu's coastal wetlands, is a paradise for birdwatchers.

Kakadu National Park is one of the brightest gems in the Northern Territory's crown of wonderful parks. The main entry to this World Heritage Area is 153 kilometres from Darwin, and the park stretches more than 200 kilometres south from the coast and along the majestic Arnhem Land Escarpment. The rains of the Wet cascade from the escarpment to flood the coastal wetlands, which become home to breeding waterbirds and many other creatures, including the Saltwater Crocodile. The traditional owners of Kakadu take an active part in the running of the area, which includes many sites of special significance to them.

Above: Outlook from a cave in the rugged escarpment, Keep River.   *Opposite:* Keep River National Park.

Keep River

It is a long, 540-kilometre drive from Katherine westwards across the Northern Territory to Keep River National Park, but the rewards are worth the effort. This stunning area of nearly 60 000 hectares on the Northern Territory-West Australian border is where the Top End meets the Kimberley.

Keep River offers staggering sandstone escarpments rising from grassy plains, on which grow bottle-trunked Boab trees and silver-trunked Ghost Gums. The hard-shelled fruits of the former provide white pith which has traditionally been bush tucker for the Aboriginal people: the fine white power which coats the bark of the latter has for thousands of years served as body paint for ceremonies. Aboriginal art sites are common in caves such as the one shown here. It is important to leave such artwork untouched – it has great significance for the traditional custodians of the land.

Nitmiluk

The deep gorges carved by the Katherine River into the Arnhem Land Plateau are the outstanding features of Nitmiluk National Park, 32 kilometres east of the town of Katherine in the Northern Territory. During the Dry, the gorges are tranquil and splendid. Cruise boats, small craft and canoes penetrate the ravines, their occupants admiring pandanus trees, ferns and paperbarks, exclaiming at birds and Freshwater Crocodiles. At this time, it is necessary to walk over the rocky bars between the final set of gorges. In the Wet, from November to March, turbulent currents swirl through the gorges.

The park is administered jointly by the traditional owners, the Jawoyn Aboriginal people, and the Parks and Wildlife Commission of the Northern Territory.

The Katherine River has slashed into the sandstone of the Arnhem Land Plateau to form a series of gorges in Nitmiluk National Park.

Lawn Hill

Lawn Hill National Park provides an oasis of cool water, green vegetation and wildlife in the far north-western corner of Queensland, about 100 kilometres west of Gregory Downs. Walking tracks allow viewing of features cut from the limestone by the creek, such as a natural dam and spa, and beautiful stretches of water framed by cabbage palms, figs and pandanus. A small area of black soil plain in the park is home to a few distinctive animals which do not usually venture into the gorge. Aborigines lived here for over 30 000 years and their artwork may be seen on the rocky walls of the gorge.

Glorious Lawn Hill Gorge, an oasis in the arid outback.

Opposite: Cradle Mountain–Lake St Clair National Park.

Above: Tropical rainforest.

MOUNTAINS AND FORESTS

Australia is an ancient land, where mountains which were once many thousands of metres high have been worn down to remnants by millions of years of erosion. The Great Dividing Range, which runs down the continent's east coast, turns towards South Australia, traps rain on its seaward side and shelters much of the country's remaining tall forest. Despite two centuries of cutting and clearing, enough of this forest remains protected in national parks to delight those who seek it out.

South West

The south-western corner of Tasmania is an area of magnificent mountain ranges and untamed rivers. For bushwalkers, nature lovers and those who wish to experience one of the few truly wild places left on the face of the planet, the Tasmanian Wilderness World Heritage Area, which includes South West National Park and the Franklin-Gordon Wild Rivers National Park, is the realisation of their dreams. Here mountains shaped by the grinding of ice sheets cradle sky-reflecting lakes, while surging rivers rush through secluded canyons and glorious forested valleys.

The stark Arthur Range, in Tasmania's south-west. Ice-carved peaks surround a sapphire-blue cirque lake.

Cradle Mountain–Lake St Clair

Above: Pandanus trees are a feature of the area known as the Ballrooms Forest.

Opposite: Lake Dove and Cradle Mountain.

One of Australia's most spectacular national parks, part of the Tasmanian Wilderness World Heritage Area, lies only 85 kilometres south of Devonport, the terminus for the ferries which cross Bass Strait from the mainland. In the north of Cradle Mountain–Lake St Clair National Park is a high, glacier-carved plateau containing 1545-metre Cradle Mountain. The centre is heathland, surrounded by peaks which include Tasmania's highest, Mt Ossa (whose summit is 1617 metres above sea level). In the south of the park is the Du Cane Range, whose streams flow eastward to Lake St Clair. The highlands of this area are noted for their plant life, particularly the ancient Antarctic Beech.

Mt Field

Seventy-three kilometres west of Hobart, capital city of Tasmania, lies Mt Field National Park, which encompasses nearly 17 000 hectares of mountainous terrain in which are stands of lush rainforest. This is one of the Island State's first-proclaimed parks, with Mt Field West the highest peak, rising to 1430 metres. The central plateau of the park is sprinkled with deep lakes in hollows gouged by ice in past ages. As in all Tasmania's parks, bushwalking is a memorable experience, with walks for people of varying levels of ability. One which is accessible to all leads to spectacular Russell Falls.

Russell Falls, Mt Field National Park.

Alpine

Above: The varnished bark of the Snow Gum protects it from heavy snowfall.

Opposite: Falls Creek, Alpine National Park.

More than 1100 native plants are found in Alpine National Park, Victoria's largest reserve, which occupies part of the Great Dividing Range in the State's north-east. In winter such natural bounty is hidden beneath the snow, but by summer the mountain slopes are bright with wildflowers. Alpine National Park includes the Bogong High Plains, Mt Bogong, Mt Buller and Mt Feathertop. Declared in 1989, the park embraces a number of ski resorts; it remains a stunning wild area, popular with bushwalkers, birdwatchers and other nature lovers, and home to the Mountain Pygmy-possum, the only marsupial to live above the snowline.

Above: The majesty of temperate rainforest.   *Opposite:* Mountain Ash, Tarra-Bulga National Park.

Tarra-Bulga

South Gippsland, south-east of Victoria's capital, Melbourne, is renowned for fertile soil and plentiful rainfall. Tarra-Bulga National Park is a small, 1520-hectare remnant of the luxuriant rainforests which once covered the Strzelecki Ranges. Its lyrebird-inhabited fern gullies and towering trees, including the fabulous Mountain Ash, make visitors wish that they could view the ranges as they were when the Polish explorer Strzelecki and his Aboriginal guide Charles Tarra knew them.

Opposite: The Balconies, a popular vantage point.　　　　　*Above*: McKenzie Falls, the Grampians.

Grampians

A series of rugged sandstone ranges, the Grampians are the final section of the Great Dividing Range. Grampians National Park, 260 kilometres north-west of Melbourne, is an area of rock faces, gorges and waterfalls. The park offers more than 160 kilometres of walking tracks, which lead to lookouts such as the Balconies (also called the Jaws of Death), Mackeys Peak and Sundial Peak. Wonderland, near the town of Halls Gap, is noted for its striking rock formations, spectacular gorges and waterfalls.

Melba Gully

Stately tree ferns border a crystal creek in Melba Gully State Park, in Victoria's Otway Ranges.

Melba Gully State Park is a 48-hectare gem nestling in the Otway Ranges, accessible from the Great Ocean Road. The reserve is noted for tree ferns and glow-worms: a eucalypt tree over 27 metres in circumference is a reminder of past glories.

Organ Pipes

As molten rock, the Organ Pipes flowed from the crater of a volcano over one million years ago. As they cooled and solidified, they cracked into columns.

The peaceful farming country of southern central Victoria was once an area of furious volcanic activity. It is a short drive from Melbourne along the Calder Highway to Organ Pipes National Park, where basalt columns are evidence of past eruptions.

Kosciusko

Kosciusko National Park encloses a large area of the New South Wales section of the Australian Alps, including Mt Kosciusko, which, at 2228 metres, is Australia's highest mountain. All of New South Wales' ski fields are inside the boundaries of this park, which extends over 600 000 hectares. During winter, Kosciusko National Park boasts a greater coverage of snow than Switzerland, and the area attracts increasing numbers of visitors. In summer when temperatures rise and mountain wildflowers bloom, bushwalking, fishing and climbing are popular.

Kosciusko National Park includes Australia's highest mountain.

Morton

Opposite: Belmore Falls cascades in stages into its gorge.

Above: Fitzroy Falls spills over cliffs of golden sandstone.

South of Sydney, east of Nowra and readily accessible from Bundanoon, Morton National Park showcases the sandstone cliffs and ravines of the Great Dividing Range. It is one of the State's largest and most spectacular national parks. The northern section has many walks and lookouts, and waterfalls such as Fitzroy, Lady Hordern, Twin and Belmore Falls, and many other attractions including Glow-worm Glen. The southern part is wild country, where the Shoalhaven, Kangaroo and Clyde Rivers have worn their way through the sandstone to the ocean. This area is a sanctuary for rare bird and mammal species.

Opposite: The Jamison Valley at dawn.   *Above*: The majestic cliffs of the Blue Mountains.

Blue Mountains

The Blue Mountains lie just west of Sydney, capital of New South Wales, and because of their rugged terrain were not crossed by Europeans until 25 years after settlement at Sydney Cove. Today Blue Mountains and Kanangra–Boyd National Parks protect much of the splendour of the sandstone walls, waterfalls and forests. The forests exhale a myriad of droplets of eucalyptus oil which reflect the rays of the sun as a blue haze. The Blue Mountains are a wonderland of natural beauty, famous also for their magnificent gardens.

Mt Kaputar

The Nandewar Range, in which stands Mt Kaputar, is the eroded remains of an enormous ancient volcano which was active around 18 million years ago.

Mt Kaputar National Park is in north central New South Wales, near the town of Narrabri. The Nandewar Range, with its rugged volcanic peaks, makes this park particularly popular with rock climbers. At least 20 of the summits stand more than 1000 metres above sea level, and a splendid panoramic view of the surrounding country is possible from Mt Kaputar, 1524 metres high.

Warrumbungle

The first European to sight the Warrumbungles, John Oxley, wrote that they were "a most stupendous range of mountains".

The stunning spires, ramparts, pinnacles and buttresses of Warrumbungle National Park rise 32 kilometres west of Coonabarabran. Its volcanic rocks were thrust from the earth in eruptions which began around the time that the Nandewar volcano, 120 kilometres to the north-west, became extinct. The park is a mecca for walkers, climbers and birdwatchers.

Opposite: Ebor Falls, on the headwaters of the Guy Fawkes River, Guy Fawkes River National Park.
Above: Apsley Falls, Oxley Wild Rivers National Park.

Guy Fawkes River and Oxley Wild Rivers

Guy Fawkes River National Park traces the course of the Guy Fawkes River across the New England Tableland of New South Wales. In the summer months, the Guy Fawkes is a favourite with whitewater rafters. Oxley Wild Rivers National Park, east of Tamworth, protects the mountain streams which contribute to the Macleay River. Around 18 kilometres east of Walcha is the rugged Apsley Falls, while Australia's highest cascade, Wollomombi Falls, is found 40 kilometres east of the city of Armidale.

Dorrigo

Opposite: Water cascades through the greenery, Dorrigo National Park.

Above: Looking out through Crystal Shower Falls.

Dorrigo is another national park whose fertile soil and scenic escarpments are the result of long-ago volcanic activity. Situated south-west of Coffs Harbour and just south-east of the town of Dorrigo, the 7900-hectare park is in mist-haunted mountains which are part of the East Coast Temperate and Subtropical Rainforest World Heritage Area. Visitors will see, in this waterfall-studded green haven, enormous buttressed trees, strangler figs, vines, ferns, orchids and a wealth of birds and other wildlife.

Above: Crows Nest Fern on rainforest vine.

Lamington

A short drive south of Brisbane, west of the Gold Coast, is Lamington National Park, which includes much of south-east Queensland's McPherson Range. It is part of the World Heritage Area which also includes Mt Warning, the Border Ranges and the Springbrook area. The park encompasses areas of subtropical rainforest, in which waterfalls, bowerbirds, the rare Albert's Lyrebird and ancient Antarctic Beech trees may be seen. There are several animals, like the Lamington Blue Cray, found only in this area. Walking tracks lead to a variety of lookouts, and to the eucalypt forests of the mountain slopes. Lamington's popular facilities are good examples of the principles of eco-tourism.

Dramatic rock formations abound in Carnarvon National Park.

Rock faces like these in Carnarvon Gorge bear stencils and engravings made by Aboriginal people.

Carnarvon

Towering Cabbage Tree Palms and Spotted Gums grow in the gorge carved by Carnarvon Creek.

The plateau in central Queensland through which Carnarvon Creek has cut the breathtaking 30-kilometre-long gorge which is the heart of Carnarvon National Park also gives rise to the streams which eventually form the Maranoa, Dawson, Warrego and Fitzroy Rivers. The park is 400 kilometres south-west of Rockhampton, but the long journey is worthwhile to experience one of Australia's most dramatic landscapes. Sandstone cliffs tower 250 metres over pools of clear water surrounded by palms, mosses and ferns. Kangaroos and possums are regular visitors to camp areas, and birdlife is abundant and colourful. Aboriginal rock art, some quite remarkable in its complexity, adorns secluded galleries. The Mt Moffatt section of the park is wilderness, a challenge to experienced adventurers.

Wooroonooran

Opposite: Tchupala Falls, Wooroonooran National Park.

Above: A strangler fig links two rainforest trees as it reaches to the sun.

Set in the Great Dividing Range between Innisfail and Cairns, north Queensland, Wooroonooran National Park amalgamates Palmerston and Bellenden Ker National Parks. The area includes the State's highest mountains, Bellenden Ker (1582 metres) and Bartle Frere (1622 metres). Because of variations in altitude, the park is home to many different sorts of vegetation, from Palmerston's lush tropical rainforests to the heathlands and mist forests found at higher altitudes. Part of the Wet Tropics World Heritage Area, this park is of incalculable importance for its plant and animal life, a wilderness of peaks, wild rivers and scenic gorges.

Opposite: Rainforest stream, Mt Lewis, North Queensland.   *Above*: Rainforest, Daintree National Park.

Daintree

The wonderful rainforests of the 56 540-hectare Daintree National Park, north-west of Mossman, Queensland, have been part of the Wet Tropics World Heritage Area since 1988. This is true tropical rainforest, mysterious and dark, shafted with golden light where a forest giant has fallen, echoing to the calls of unseen birds foraging in the canopy far overhead. Small, clear creeks rush through the forest to their meetings with larger streams, which finally flow into the Daintree or other rivers, and then into the blue Coral Sea.

Stirling Range

Above: The awesome profile of the Stirling Range at dawn.   *Opposite:* In spring, Stirling Range National Park is wildflower territory.

The Stirling Range rises from the coastal plain north of Albany, Western Australia. Stirling Range National Park, over 115 500 hectares in area, is famous for its prolific springtime display of wildflowers, and for the birds and small mammals which feast on the nectar produced by the wealth of blossoms.

Climbers revel in the challenge presented by peaks such as Bluff Knoll, Ellen Peak and Toolbrunup, all over 1000 metres high. The range is cold and windswept in winter, but in spring and summer it is a delightful place to walk, camp and observe the natural beauty.

Leeuwin–Naturaliste and Walpole–Nornalup

Opposite: Nornalup Inlet, Walpole–Nornalup National Park.　　　　　*Above*: Regrowth Karri forest, Leeuwin–Naturaliste National Park.

Leeuwin–Naturaliste National Park stretches down the coast of Western Australia from 270 kilometres south of Perth, between the two capes jutting from the continent's south-west corner. Behind the park's spectacular headlands and beaches are forested valleys, where orchids carpet the ground in spring and the advance scouts of the towering Karri trees of the extreme south-west can be seen. Walpole–Nornalup National Park covers 18 116 hectares around these two southern inlets. It offers beaches and calm estuaries which are a holiday-maker's paradise, and magnificent forests of Karri and Red Tingle, the latter showcased in the Valley of the Giants.

Above: The enchantment of William Bay National Park, WA.　　*Opposite*: Torndirrup National Park, WA.

THE EVER-CHANGING COAST

Some of Australia's most memorable national parks are to be found along its 36 000 kilometres of coastline. The striking coastal scenery may be formed by the ocean's continual battle with the land, which it wears away by brute force, or undermines subtly so that the solid rock, like a martial arts opponent, is defeated by its own weight and strength. It may also be the result of active creation, like the Great Barrier Reef, whose immense structure is the result of thousands of years of home-building by tiny, soft-bodied coral animals. Either way, coastal landscapes are never static, always in flux.

Jardine River

Jardine River National Park is near the tip of Cape York Peninsula and is noted for unique plants as well as plentiful wildlife.

Queensland's Jardine River National Park encompasses a large part of the catchment of the Jardine River, in the north of Cape York Peninsula. It is 235 000 hectares in extent, and contains areas of rare vine forest as well as an area called the Wet Desert, a wetlands area where insectivorous plants and other interesting flora can be seen. Jardine River National Park, like much of the Cape, is Saltwater Crocodile country.

Cape Melville

Behind the shore, granite boulders are strewn across the foothills of the Melville Range, Cape Melville National Park.

Cape Melville National Park is on the eastern side of the base of Cape York Peninsula, Queensland. It has a coastline of granite headlands and delightful sandy beaches and extends for 42 000 hectares to enclose most of Cape Melville. Near the tip of the cape is a memorial to more than 300 people who died when a cyclone devastated a pearling fleet moored in Bathurst Bay in 1899.

The Great Barrier Reef

The Great Barrier Reef stretches for 2000 kilometres along the coast of Queensland. It covers 34.87 million hectares of the Coral Sea and Pacific Ocean, and is made up of over 2500 individual reefs and over 70 coral cays and islands. In 1975, the Great Barrier Reef Marine Park Authority was set up to oversee this incredible structure, based on the stony cases made by tiny coral animals over thousands of years. The Reef was proclaimed a World Heritage Area in 1981.

The Great Barrier Reef is one of the world's few remaining unspoiled tropical coral reefs, a vast concourse of living organisms, amazing in their variety and fascinating in their interactions. The area is a mecca for both tourists and students of marine life, with unlimited opportunities to explore, discover, or just relax.

Lady Musgrave Island surrounded by its lagoon and outer reef.

Cape Tribulation reaches out into the sea, Cape Tribulation National Park.

Rainforest covers the slopes of the mountains near Cape Tribulation.

Magnificent Fan Palms are an admired feature of Cape Tribulation National Park.

Cape Tribulation

Cape Tribulation was named by Captain James Cook in 1770, after his sturdy barque the *Endeavour* was damaged on a coral reef just to the north. The ship was repaired, Cook sailed away to fame, and today Cape Tribulation is renowned as one of Australia's most beautiful tropical national parks, where the emerald-forested mountains fall dramatically to the sapphire waters of the Coral Sea. A particularly breathtaking part of the Wet Tropics World Heritage Area, this is where the rainforest meets the Great Barrier Reef.

Above: Mangroves and tidal creeks, Missionary Bay.   *Opposite:* Hillock Point, Hinchinbrook Island.

Hinchinbrook Island

The North Queensland town of Cardwell is the gateway to Hinchinbrook Island, a wonderful wilderness island whose granite Mt Bowen rises 1142 metres from the ocean. Hinchinbrook Island National Park protects all the island's 39 350 hectares and is the world's largest island national park. On the north and west sides are extensive mangrove swamps and, further inland, stands of tropical rainforest. On the eastern side, where rainfall is lower, there are eucalypt forests, long sandy beaches and secluded bays. The Thorsborne Trail allows walkers to enjoy the eastern coast, from Ramsay Bay to Zoe Bay, with its beautiful waterfall, then on to George Point, at the island's southern tip.

85

Whitsunday Islands

Above: Hill Inlet, Whitsunday Islands National Park.

Opposite: This is sailors' heaven.

The 100-odd islands which make up the Whitsunday Group are in the Whitsunday Passage, off the coast of Queensland, and form an unequalled 160 kilometres of magic Coral Sea gems. A number of these rugged continental islands form Whitsunday Islands National Park, their summits crowned with forests and their shores girdled with marvellous beaches. Some of these contain undeveloped wilderness, while others are host to popular holiday resorts. The reefs fringing the islands are rich in marine life, though the Great Barrier Reef lies out to sea.

Great Sandy

The world's largest sand island, Fraser Island lies off the coast of southern Queensland. Over one-third of the island lies within Great Sandy National Park and the entire island, 184 000 hectares, is listed as a World Heritage Area. Winds carried sand from the area now known as New South Wales and deposited it off the coast of south-east Queensland during the ice age, creating and shaping the island. The land breeze then carried soil on which plant seeds germinated and grew, stabilising the sand and creating unique heathland and rainforest communities.

The Aboriginal people knew Fraser Island as *K'gari*, meaning "the best possible country". Its scenic delights include cliff-faces of coloured sands, towering sand dunes, over 40 remarkable dune lakes and crystalline rainforest streams.

Features of Fraser Island include sand dunes, heathland and perched lakes.

Lord Howe Island

Above: Balls Pyramid is over 500 metres high.   *Opposite:* Lord Howe Island is noted for spectacular peaks and magnificent beaches.

Seven hundred kilometres north-east of Sydney, the Lord Howe Island Group is part of New South Wales. Inscribed on the World Heritage List in 1982, this is a subtropical haven with a permanent population of under 300 and at most 400 visitors at any one time. Lord Howe, the Admiralty Islands, and the massive Balls Pyramid, 23 kilometres south of Lord Howe, were forced above the ocean by volcanic activity around 7 000 000 years ago. Today, Lord Howe is an idyllic holiday destination, with rainforests, mountains, coral reefs and over 168 species of birds awaiting discovery by those lucky enough to visit.

Jervis Bay National Park encompasses the headland forming the southern boundary of the bay.

Crowdy Bay National Park, just south of Port Macquarie, is noted for dramatic scenery and plentiful birdlife.

Coastal parks of NSW

The coast of New South Wales has a large resident population and is a favoured place for holiday-makers. It is a tribute to far-sighted planners, who realised the importance of preserving fragile coastal habitats, that so much has been reserved in national parks. Together, they preserve 1400 kilometres of beaches.

Australia's first national park, Royal National Park, is south of Sydney, and provides wild coastal spaces for city dwellers; Jervis Bay National Park, on the South Coast, protects splendid scenery and wonderful marine life; and Crowdy Bay National Park, on the State's northern coast, protects beaches, rock formations and pools, and rugged cliffs.

Semi-detached Point and South Era Beach, Royal National Park, south of Sydney.

Wilsons Promontory

Above: Admiring the view from Mt Oberon.

Opposite: South-East Point and lighthouse, Wilsons Promontory.

Wilsons Promontory National Park covers the southernmost part of the Australian mainland. The Prom is a granite massif jutting into Bass Strait, with sheltered beaches tucked between the rocky headlands; behind the shore, the mountain slopes and valleys are covered with flowering heaths. The park extends over 49 000 hectares and there are more than 80 kilometres of walking tracks: two of the most popular are the trek to the summit of Mt Oberon and the stroll along the Lilly Pilly Gully Nature Walk. The waters surrounding the inlets and coves of the Prom are also protected as marine reserves and are popular for scuba diving and sailing.

Port Campbell

Above: Muttonbird Island is a breeding sanctuary for seabirds.   *Opposite:* Two of the famous Twelve Apostles, Port Campbell National Park.

Port Campbell National Park covers about 1750 hectares along the coast of Victoria, and is around 250 kilometres south-west of Melbourne. The Twelve Apostles, Muttonbird Island and London Bridge, like many other features of the park, have been produced by the relentless Southern Ocean pounding away softer parts of the coastline, leaving harder stacks freestanding. This is the notorious Shipwreck Coast, where many vessels, such as the famous *Loch Ard,* came to grief on rocks and reefs. Access to Port Campbell National Park is by the Great Ocean Road, which was hewn from the limestone coastal cliffs by soldiers returned from World War I.

South West Cape, South West National Park.

Tasmania's South West National Park includes some of the world's finest remaining wilderness areas.

South West

A wilderness of mountain ranges, wild river systems and rugged coastline, South West National Park covers 605 000 hectares in Tasmania's south-western corner. Scenically grand and biologically diverse, the park forms part of the Tasmanian Wilderness World Heritage Area, home to the rare Huon Pine and to superb stands of cool temperate rainforest. This is a bushwalker's dream, where vivid wildflowers appear magically each springtime and every turn of the trail brings in to view new natural wonders.

Flinders Chase

Above: Admirals Arch, Cape du Couedic, Flinders Chase National Park.

Opposite: Remarkable Rocks are eroded granite boulders.

South Australia's Kangaroo Island is separated from the mainland by the narrow Backstairs Passage. The entire western part of the island, 73 920 hectares of mallee-covered sandy country, eucalypt-forested plateau and rugged coastline, form Flinders Chase National Park and Ravine des Casoars Wilderness Protection Area. The island is home to many native animals, including species rare on, or vanishing from, the mainland. Kangaroos, emus, echidnas and koalas are popular favourites, while a breeding colony of rare Australian Sea-lions is an attraction at Seal Bay Conservation Park, on the south coast of the island. Kangaroo Island is easily accessible by air from Adelaide, or by car ferry from Cape Jervis.

Nullarbor

Nullarbor is Latin for "no trees", but the vegetation on the plain supports a variety of birds and other creatures.

The Eyre Highway runs through Nullarbor National Park, which occupies the extreme south-western corner of South Australia. To the south are the sheer Bunda Cliffs, stretching 200 kilometres from just past the Western Australian border to the Head of the Bight. All around are treeless plains under which are labyrinths of limestone caves, many unexplored.

A shimmering stretch of sea and sand in Coffin Bay National Park.

Coffin Bay

Forty-six kilometres from Port Lincoln, South Australia, is one of Australia's finest coastal reserves. Coffin Bay National Park contains 28 106 hectares and covers the Coffin Bay Peninsula. The bay gained its unusual name when explorer Matthew Flinders honoured his friend Sir Isaac Coffin. Once the location of many shipwrecks, this rugged coastline also holds marvellous stretches of sand, notably Almonta Beach, a prize amongst beaches. This is great country for those who wish to explore, adventure and experience an exceptional coastal wilderness area.

Two Peoples Bay Nature Reserve, near Albany.

Cape Le Grand National Park, near Esperance.

Shelley Beach, Torbay Bay, West Cape Howe National Park, near Denmark.

The Salmon Holes, Flinders Peninsula, Torndirrup National Park, near Albany.

The southern coast of Western Australia

A headland in Fitzgerald River National Park, between Albany and Esperance.

The southern coastline of Western Australia, from Augusta to the South Australian border, is full of striking contrasts. Rugged granite headlands shelter tiny coves; multicoloured cliffs tower over long beaches of white sand. In some places coastal heathlands run down to the beach, their grey-greens and silver-blues disappearing in a blaze of flowers in springtime.

The national parks along this coastline are dramatic, the Southern Ocean crashing against their rocky headlands each winter. During the rest of the year, fishing, sailing, and bushwalking are enjoyed by holiday-makers.

Zuytdorp Cliffs and François Peron

Above: The majestic Zuytdorp Cliffs, a protected area.

Opposite: François Peron National Park is part of the Shark Bay World Heritage Area.

The Zuytdorp Cliffs stretch up the coast of Western Australia north of Kalbarri, and are named after the Dutch ship, wrecked here in 1712. François Peron National Park comprises 40 000 hectares of the Peron Peninsula, which juts into Shark Bay. The area is notable for its landlocked gypsum lakes and its wildlife, including the Dugongs of the bay, and is famous for its Bottlenose Dolphins, which regularly come into the shallow waters off Monkey Mia to interact with humans.

Mudflats, mangroves and a flat-topped hill known locally as a jump-up, in Prince Regent Nature Reserve, the Kimberley.

Prince Regent

The Prince Regent River flows in a straight line for more than 100 kilometres through a long crack in the sandstone of the remote western Kimberley in Western Australia. Most of this area can be accessed only from the sea, with due regard to the extreme rise and fall of local tides. The Prince Regent Nature Reserve contains over half the wildlife species found in the entire Kimberley, as well as 500 plant species. This is a fragile wilderness area and its watercourses, rainforests and jagged gorges may also harbour animals as yet unknown to science.

Sandstone formations in the proposed Limmen Gate National Park.

Limmen Gate

The proposed Limmen Gate National Park would protect a stunning area of remarkable sandstone formations in the Tawallah Range, in the south-west of the Gulf of Carpentaria. This country is most easily seen from the air, though the full effect of the 20 to 50 metre columns can be appreciated only from the ground. Waterways leading to the gulf provide feeding grounds for a variety of wildlife. Like all northern parts of Australia, this wild area is best travelled in the Dry, from May to September.

Australia's national parks are popular areas for learning about the environment and for enjoyment. Care must be taken to preserve their ecosystems and natural beauty.

Caring about national parks

The Gordon River, Franklin–Gordon Wild Rivers National Park, Tasmania.

Some national parks, and particular areas of certain parks, are more fragile than others. The wellbeing of any national park depends on the care taken by the people using it, and easily damaged places, such as coastal dunes, desert waterholes, coral reefs and fragile rock formations, need protection, even from their keenest admirers. If you are enjoying a national park, it is important to stay on marked tracks, camp at designated sites, wash away from watercourses and carry out all rubbish. All native plants and animals are protected in parks and pets are not allowed within their boundaries.

Australia's national parks are precious reserves for everyone to enjoy, so take a photograph for your memories and leave no trace of your visit.

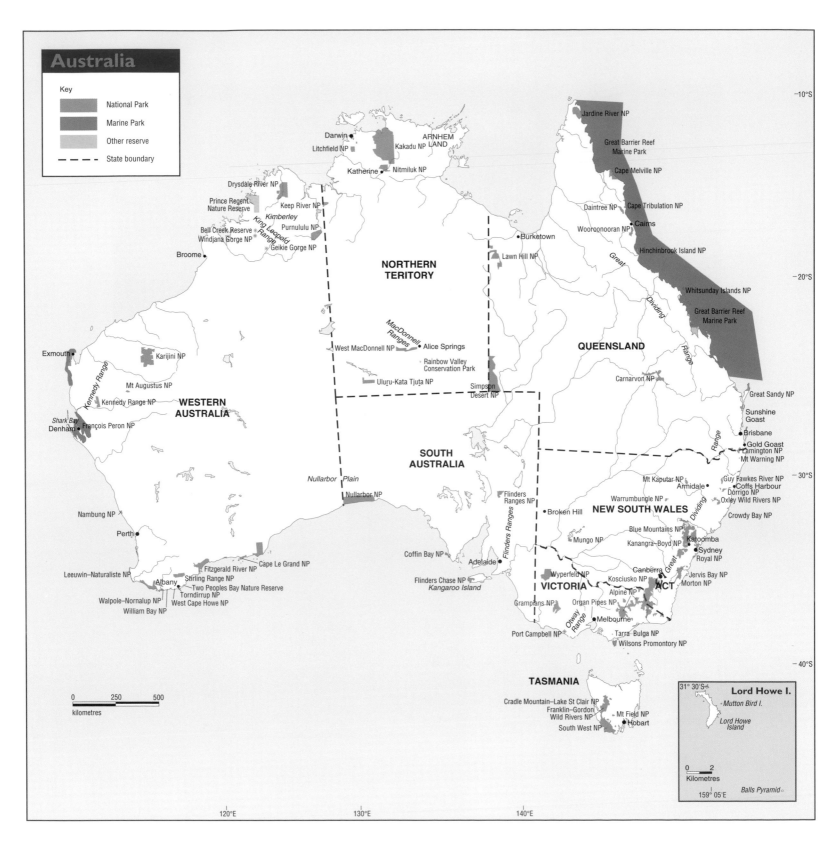

Australia

Key
- National Park
- Marine Park
- Other reserve
- - - - State boundary

Darwin
ARNHEM LAND
Litchfield NP
Kakadu NP
Katherine
Nitmiluk NP
Jardine River NP
Great Barrier Reef Marine Park
Cape Melville NP
Daintree NP
Cape Tribulation NP
Wooroonooran NP
Cairns
Hinchinbrook Island NP

Drysdale River NP
Prince Regent Nature Reserve
Keep River NP
Kimberley
Purnululu NP
Bell Creek Reserve
Windjana Gorge NP
King Leopold Range
Geikie Gorge NP
Broome

NORTHERN TERITORY

Burketown
Lawn Hill NP

Whitsunday Islands NP
Great Barrier Reef Marine Park

Exmouth
Karijini NP
Mt Augustus NP
Kennedy Range
Kennedy Range NP

MacDonnell Ranges
West MacDonnell NP
Alice Springs
Rainbow Valley Conservation Park
Uluru-Kata Tjuta NP
Simpson Desert NP

QUEENSLAND

Carnarvon NP
Great Sandy NP
Sunshine Goast
Brisbane
Gold Goast
Lamington NP
Mt Warning NP

WESTERN AUSTRALIA

Shark Bay
Denham
François Peron NP

SOUTH AUSTRALIA

Nullarbor Plain
Nullarbor NP

Flinders Ranges NP
Broken Hill
Warrumbungle NP
Mt Kaputar NP
Armidale
Guy Fawkes River NP
Coffs Harbour
Dorrigo NP
Oxley Wild Rivers NP

NEW SOUTH WALES

Crowdy Bay NP

Nambung NP
Perth

Mungo NP
Blue Mountains NP
Katoomba
Kanangra-Boyd NP
Sydney
Royal NP

Coffin Bay NP
Adelaide

Great Dividing Range

Leeuwin-Naturaliste NP
Fitzgerald River NP
Cape Le Grand NP
Albany
Stirling Range NP
Two Peoples Bay Nature Reserve
Torndirrup NP
West Cape Howe NP
Walpole-Nornalup NP
William Bay NP

Flinders Chase NP
Kangaroo Island

Wyperfeld NP
Canberra
Jervis Bay NP
Kosciusko NP
Morton NP
ACT

VICTORIA

Grampians NP
Organ Pipes NP
Otway Range
Melbourne
Alpine NP

Port Campbell NP
Tarra Bulga NP
Wilsons Promontory NP

TASMANIA

Cradle Mountain-Lake St Clair NP
Franklin-Gordon Wild Rivers NP
Mt Field NP
Hobart
South West NP

0 250 500
kilometres

Lord Howe I.
31° 30'S
Mutton Bird I.
Lord Howe Island

0 2
Kilometres
159° 05'E
Balls Pyramid

120°E   130°E   140°E

-10°S
-20°S
-30°S
-40°S

Exploring national parks

Australia has an incredible variety of landscapes in its national parks, and as interest in wild places has grown, access to even the most geographically remote reserves has been improved. An overseas visitor can arrive at any international airport in Australia and within a few hours travel by air to the wonders of Uluṟu–Kata Tjuṯa or West MacDonnell National Parks, both in the centre of the continent. There are few national parks which cannot be reached in a conventional vehicle at most times of the year, though during the Wet many places in the tropical north are inaccessible because of flooded rivers.

For those who wish to camp, many parks have caravan sites and campsites; for those who like their comforts, accommodation can be found within a short distance of most scenic parks. Though bushwalkers and climbers enjoy the challenges of national parks, the less energetic majority can find peaceful activities, and many reserves provide good facilities for nature lovers with disabilities. There are many guidebooks and brochures offering advice on how to get the best from a national park experience, and park rangers are sources of friendly information. It's a great way to see the real Australia.

Steve Parish

World-famous photographer Steve Parish began his remarkable career by recording marine life off Australia's coasts. After discovering the fascinations of the rainforest and its wild creatures, he has spent much of his life journeying around Australia photographing the landscapes, plants, animals and the people of the land. Of recent years, he has extended the range of his subjects to include Australia's cities and towns.

The magnificent library of images which has resulted has become the heart of Steve Parish Publishing Pty Ltd. Through the firm's publications, Steve and his wife and partner Jan are realising their dream of sharing Australia with the world.

Celebrating Australia is a collection of titles which present the incomparable beauty of the southern continent in superb photographs and text. As Steve comments: "After a lifetime of travel and asking questions, I have only just begun to discover how much there is to learn about Australia. I hope these books arouse in others a desire like mine to explore and to appreciate this wonderful country."

Index

First published by Steve Parish Publishing Pty Ltd, 1997
PO Box 2160, Fortitude Valley BC, Queensland 4006, Australia
© copyright Steve Parish Publishing Pty Ltd, 1997

ISBN 1 875932 94 1

Photography: Steve Parish
Text: Pat Slater, Steve Parish Publishing, Australia

Map supplied by MAPgraphics
Editing, design: Steve Parish Publishing, Australia
Printed in Hong Kong
Colour separations by Steve Parish Publishing, Australia